S0-ARN-735

Focus or Fail

50 Tips for Organizing Your Stuff, Prioritizing Your Activities, and Becoming More Effective

By Steve Norton

www.SteveNortonPM.com

steve@SteveNortonPM.com

Also by Steve Norton

Steve Norton is a co-author of the Amazon.com best-seller *The Success Secret: The World's Leading Experts Reveal Their Secrets for Success in Business and in Life*. Co-written with Jack Canfield and featuring leading experts from around the world, the book offers an inspiring collection of success stories and practical advice for optimizing your potential and achieving your health, wealth, personal and business goals. To purchase this best-seller, go to www.SteveNortonPM.com.

"Steve Norton is a master of strategic organization and planning and Focus or Fail will become your product/project development bible! Time is money. As a serial entrepreneur and small business owner, I know the challenge of "grow or fail" hinges on organization and planning. Agility plus swift execution of innovative products and services is key to a healthy bottom line. I count on Steve Norton to guide my businesses with tools and strategies to keep all our product development on track without missing a beat. If you've ever dropped the ball or been late to market...after learning Steve's systems - NEVER again."
Lynden L Kidd, JD, Tucson, Arizona
Conscious Entrepreneur, Talent Scout, Business and Career Strategist, Professional Speaker & Corporate Trainer
www.lyndenkidd.com and www.nextiteration.net

"Three things strike me about Steve Norton: 1) his humility, 2) his passion for helping others and 3) his ability to identify and obliterate obstacles with his clear blueprints. Using his 30 years of hard-earned experience from the complex nuclear industry, Steve provides 50 simple tips to quickly improve your ability to plan, organize, and execute anything. This is the kind of book you'll buy for yourself, and then – before you know it – you'll wind up buying copies to give to your employees, clients and friends. It's that practical."
Dr. Danny Brassell
America's Leading Reading Ambassador and Founder of *The Lazy Readers' Book Club* www.dannybrassell.com and www.lazyreaders.com

"If you carry just one book around with you, this is the one! Steve shows you 50 simple ways to improve your clarity, better organize your competing priorities, and get more of the right things done fast. This book will change the way you look at things and what you accomplish for the rest of your life! Organization is not my strong suit. That said, and I read a lot on organization to find the magic bullet – in reading Steve's book, I gleaned many ideas that I can put into use."
Elise Lacher, Seminole, Florida
Strategic Veterinary Consulting, Inc.

About the Author

Steve Norton is one of the most highly rated international instructors and speakers in his field of project management. He is a business advisor, enthusiastically sharing his expertise for organizing, planning and executing complex projects. He is a trainer and motivator, dedicated to helping people become more effective and achieve greater success.

Steve Norton gained his project management credentials through a 30-year career in the nuclear industry. As a senior manager for Fortune 500 companies, he directed project management activities, strategic planning, financial planning, scheduling, plant operations, and facility startups. He managed large nuclear waste processing facilities and was the project manager for award-winning fast-track projects. He was responsible for portfolios of projects valued in the hundreds of millions of dollars. Turning his expertise to commercial enterprise, he launched several profitable companies.

In 2010, he established Project Management Skills, LLC and became a Project Management Institute (PMI)® Registered Education Provider (R.E.P.)®. Through his business, he provides project management training that prepares business professionals for the Project Management Professional (PMP)® certification exam. His popular Boot Camps are revered for his upbeat presentation style. Students credit his thorough instruction for helping them pass the exam and earn the coveted PMP® certification.

PMP, PMI, R.E.P. are registered marks of the Project Management Institute, Inc.

Steve offers a unique perspective from a diverse background and a lifelong study of success principles and best practices. He has trained with America's #1 Success Coach, Jack Canfield, co-creator of the *Chicken Soup for the Soul* book series and author of the best-selling book, *The Success Principles*. Working with Jack, Steve has assisted in training students in the success principles and is featured in Jack's acclaimed instructional videos along with James Malinchak (author and star of ABC television's hit series, *Secret Millionaire, Season One)* and Timothy Ferris (author of *The 4-Hour Work Week*).

Steve has a Master of Sciences degree in Project Management from Boston University and a Project Management Professional (PMP)® certification from the Project Management Institute . He is actively involved with regional PMI® chapters throughout the nation, which repeatedly offer his PMP® exam prep Boot Camps to their members for professional development.

Steve lives in the Pacific Northwest with his wife Denise Ciarlo. He is a long-time volunteer in his local community, including leadership in the PMI® chapter.

For more information visit SteveNortonPM.com or email Steve at steve@SteveNortonPM.com.

Praise for Project Management Skills, LLC Boot Camps and Training Workshops

"Steve —Thanks for your help in passing the class. The exam prep class was key to helping me get ready!"
Steve Abarta, PMP
Yakima, Washington

"Excellent opportunity to provide focus on transforming goals into actionable steps, identify how to break through personal limitations, and achieve personal success."
Jeff Markillie

"Steve Norton makes the class comfortable and fun. He makes you look a little deeper at what you want and how to go about getting it. Thanks for a great insightful class."
Allie Reaka

"This PMP class was excellent! I'm amazed at how much material we covered in 3 days. I learned a lot and would highly recommend the course. Steve Norton was an outstanding instructor – very knowledgeable."
Angie Rhyne, PNNL
Richland, Washington

"Have always enjoyed Steve's courses; he "cuts to the chase" while providing useful information. This course was not 'just another nuts and bolts' course but probes the whats and whys of both project management and life."
Bob Birney

"Thanks again for all the support and mentoring you provided to the PMP Boot Camp class in June. I passed the PMP Exam on the first try."
Russell Looney, PMP
Tri-Cities, Washington

"We are very grateful to have had Steve be a keynote speaker at our PD Day in Victoria! We learned from him that risk planning and management, a topic many times misunderstood and fuzzy, is not that difficult at all! Steve showed us with clear and simple techniques and examples how to overcome and work through client objections to investing in risk management planning efforts."
Calin Somosan
Victoria, British Columbia, Canada

"I am strongly recommending Steve Norton's PMP Boot Camp. I took the 3 day course, spent 2 days taking the included online tests and passed the exam a week later. Steve presents the material in a manner which encourages retention, and the class was actually very enjoyable. Thanks Steve!"
Dave Wallace, PMP, EVP
D. Gerard Consulting, LLC

"I signed up for this class (Success Principles) with the primary motive of earning PDU's toward my PMP re-certification. What I found after a few minutes in the class was that I'm glad I picked this class. It was meaningful on several levels for me and I believe the class message is an important one for life in general, as well as work life."
Everett Orr

"I am writing to let you know that I have passed the PMP exam and obtained the Project Management Professional (PMP)® Credential. Very exciting for me to have achieved this goal! Thank you very much for your help, your class was very helpful. After the class, I really had a good understanding of how the knowledge areas, process groups, and processes fit together. I'm glad I had the opportunity to take your PMP boot camp, and the Velociteach materials were perfect to help me study and remember all the details. Thanks for everything."
David DelSordo, PMP
USDA Forest Service

"My investment in the 3-day class was well worth it. There is no way I would have prepared properly without the class. I would highly recommend and endorse this class for anyone planning to take the PMP exam. Thanks, Steve. Your class was informative, fun and effective!"
Wade Zinnecker, PMP
Billings, Montana

"Last Thursday... I passed the PMP Exam. I want to start by thanking you for your excellent tutelage. The boot camp was my initial, formal introduction to the material. The class provided the essential foundation to build upon during my studies. Thank you again for the opportunity to learn from you, and the wonderful tips to pass the exam. Literally, I wouldn't have passed without you. I hope our paths cross again."
Nathan Bartow, PMP

"Excellent class to prep for PMP test and to meet and share PM concepts with other project managers. Perfect complement to real-world experience! Helps to standardize terminology and provides a framework for understanding and thinking about and planning projects."
Frank Guendelsberger
Energy Northwest, Richland, Washington

"... I passed the PMP exam. Your class was indispensable in helping me achieve a passing grade... Thank you again for the wonderful class and support."
Bob Finstad, PMP

"Steve is able to cut to the heart of the matter with compassion to provide constructive, insightful coaching that encourages you to take action. Leveraging his significant background in project management, he brings added value with his natural ability to support you with developing a plan that drives results."
Nathalie Osborn
Discover Your Own Renewable Energy Portland, Oregon

"I highly recommend Steve as a very effective trainer for PMP/CAPM exam preparation class delivery. He continues to deliver outstanding training for our PMI Chapter and we continue to re-hire him for all our PMP/CAPM exam prep training. I have also had the opportunity to see Steve in action at PMI conferences. He has a unique ability to adapt his teaching to his audience and yet deliver the messages he needs to get across."
Dale Matheson, PMP
President, PMI Montana Chapter

"The methods used to get us all interacting, and to have us work with many of the attendees were great! Very effective."
Matt Strong

Dedication

This book is dedicated to Bill Norton, my mentor and father who taught me through his example that we can do anything we choose. And he *could* do anything!

To Paula Henry (Norton), my friend and little sister who was brilliant beyond her education and wise beyond her years. And what a fantastic sense of humor!

To Kathy Norton, my big sister, confidant and so much more. You touched so many lives with your caring and thoughtful ways.

I love you and sure miss your smiling faces.

Acknowledgements

Thank you to my wise, supportive friend and wife Denise Ciarlo, who has been behind me 100% in everything I do • to a great coach, James Malinchak, who pushed me to "GSDF – Get Stuff Done Fast!" • to a great mentor Jack Canfield who helped me fully understand I create my outcomes (and by the way, so do you) • to a good friend and fellow master mind partner Ricardo Garcia who helped provide organization to this book. I also acknowledge the many other family members, friends, and associates who have guided, pushed, and taught me over the years.

How to Use This Book

I know you are busy and often it is difficult to find the time for reading a thick book and then assimilating all the information into your daily routines. This book is thin and to the point for that reason.

Most of these tips are stand alone, that is, you can read one and do it without regard to the others. A few are follow ups to other tips, but those will be clear when you read them. Feel free to go directly to the tips that will serve you now. Some people will want to read all the way through the book once then return to those tips they want to apply now.

Each tip has a few questions to answer or actions to take, which will start you down that path to greater effectiveness. I suggest you do them as you read the book – Yes, it's OK to write in the book. The knowledge is useless unless you put it into practice.

Everyone is at a different place in his or her personal and professional development. You may be excelling in one or several areas, and those tips will be less useful to you. One precaution – be aware that we frequently work on the things we're good at because they're easier and more comfortable. So if you rule out trying a tip, make sure it's because you've truly mastered that area, not because it puts you further out of your comfort zone.

Set a goal to embody, try, practice, or apply one or more tips each week. You don't need to drown in everything at once, just lean into it. Most importantly, have fun. You will get good at things, but never great, unless you have fun doing them.

"If you think you can do it, or you think you can't do it, you are right."

— Henry Ford

Contents

Clarification

Goal Setting

Planning

Action

Management

Risk Management

Readiness

NOTES

1. Define what success will look like

Before starting anything, think about what success will look like. Sometimes "complete the project" seems pretty clear, but is completion the only measure of success? What else matters?

If you're giving a talk to a group, for example, decide up front what success will look like. When it's over, do you want them to know something new? Do you want them to take action? Do you want to inspire them to take on a new challenge? Or do you want them to give you feedback for improving the presentation?

Make a list early on of what is included and what is not included in successful completion of your project or activity. Include all the elements, especially if they're small, because often we take small things for granted.

If you're entering into an agreement with another party, early in the process discuss the definition of success with them so it's a shared definition. For example, if you are working on a complex project, are you acquiring each permit, writing acceptance tests, writing operational tests, issuing test reports, writing maintenance procedures, keying the doors, developing operating and emergency procedures and issuing final reports, or will some of these tasks be the responsibility of others? Different industries have different norms, as do different companies within industries. The people you are dealing with may have different experiences and expectations. Your standard practice may not be theirs. A clear and shared definition of success is a smart step to accomplishment.

Pick one thing you're working on and ask yourself: What does success look like? What's included or not included in the finished project? Who needs to agree up front with your definition of success? Set a deadline for getting the agreement.

NOTES

2. Ask the important questions

Why am I doing this? Am I getting what I expected? Is it worth it?

These three questions are just as important for personal undertakings as they are for business projects. For example, you may have become a leader of your child's scout troop because you wanted to spend quality time with your child and model good behavior. However, after two years, you find yourself on the scout's advisory board, heading up the summer camp, and leading the fund-raising committee. You may be spending 16 hours a month on scouts, and only 4 hours is quality time with your son or daughter. It may be time to step back and ask: Why am I doing this? Am I getting what I expected from it? Is it worth it?

Your answers to these important questions can help you evaluate your activities relative to your reasons and expectations for getting involved. You could decide to continue as a troop leader, spending 4 hours per month with your scout, but reallocate the other 12 hours of scouting commitments into other activities that give you more direct time with your child. Just like in projects, *scope creep* can expand and impact our personal activities. Asking the important questions can help you redirect your time for activities that actually help you achieve your goals.

Pick one of your undertakings and ask yourself: Why am I doing it? What do I hope to get from it? Am I getting what I expected? Is it everything or only partially what I expected? Am I getting things I didn't expect?

Is it worth it? (Given what I'm putting out, is the return commensurate?) What, if anything, am I going to change?

NOTES

Health and well being

Wealth, income, savings, earnings

Personal development or spiritual growth

3. Focus on what, not how

As you set goals and objectives, focus on the end result. What do you want to accomplish? Don't limit yourself by thoughts such as: How will I ever achieve that? How can we do that, since we've never done that before? Focusing on the HOW keeps you in the same box and limits your results. To really excel, to achieve great things, decide WHAT you want to do and let the how come later.

I once volunteered to lead a national fundraising campaign at our plant of 900 people. The annual campaign typically raised about $3,000 through bake sales, auctions, luncheons, etc. At the first team meeting, I asked what we wanted to accomplish, how much money we wanted to raise. The team suggested we achieve what had been done in the past. I challenged them to set a wildly ridiculous goal of raising $10,000. The conversation immediately turned to: How will we do that? How can we possibly raise $10,000 when we've raised only $3,000 in the past?

Not knowing how we would do it, we went public with our goal to raise $10,000, and the ideas just started pouring in. One idea was to create a 100 X 100 Club in which 100 people would donate $100 each. With that approach, company matching funds, and other ideas, we raised over $10,000. We found new ways to raise the money and set a new bar for the annual campaign. If we had bogged down in the HOW right out of the gate, we never would have set and achieved such an ambitious goal.

Without regard to HOW, list a couple of lofty goals for each of the following (more detail in Tips 5 and 6):
- *Health and well being*
- *Wealth, income, savings, earnings*
- *Personal development or spiritual growth*

NOTES

4. Begin with the end

An important difference between those who are efficient and those who are effective is that effective people have a clear awareness of the end result. Identify what you are trying to accomplish in a situation. What will it look like when you are done?

In my neighborhood I saw an enterprising man going from door to door putting a piece of paper on each door handle. He really had the process down, and he was zipping efficiently up and down each cul-de-sac. Later, I saw he was distributing a well written, to-the-point, offer to mow lawns and pick up leaves.

However, in my neighborhood all residents pay a monthly homeowners association fee which includes all the lawn mowing and yard maintenance. The man was efficient at getting out his message but he was not effective in creating new business because the message was delivered to the wrong audience. He was efficient but not effective because he didn't have a clear picture of the end result. The goal was to acquire 10 new customers, not distribute 100 fliers.

Identify something that is very important to you right now. Think about what success looks like at the end. Make sure it's the outcome you want like 10 new customers, not the action you will take like deliver 100 fliers. Once you have a very clear picture of the successful outcome, write it down. Then, you can screen all proposed actions to see if they are truly effective in leading to your desired outcome.

NOTES

_____

_____

_____

_____

_____

_____

_____

_____

_____

_____

_____

_____

_____

_____

_____

_____

_____

_____

_____

_____

_____

_____

_____

_____

_____

_____

_____

_____

_____

_____

5. Set audacious goals and negotiate rewards

Michelangelo said, *"The greater danger for most of us is not that our aim is too high and we miss it, but that it is too low and we reach it."*

Why not set an audacious goal? Usually the answer (whether you are willing to admit it or not) is that we are afraid to publicly declare a big goal for fear of looking stupid if we don't achieve it. What if you set a goal to triple your income next year and you failed? You only doubled it. Would you feel stupid and be disappointed? Probably not, doubling your income would be great!

If your crew normally built a custom home (or developed a new product) in six months, what would it be worth to you if they built the next one (to the same standards) in three months? It could be worth a lot in avoided wages, reduced interest on capital investment, and quicker return on investment from the earlier sale. What would it be worth to the crew to complete the construction or development in three months instead of six? You could work with your crew to set an audacious goal and negotiate an incredible incentive to reward their success. For example, you could offer them a week's paid vacation or whatever would be meaningful to them. It could be a great bonus for them and a worthwhile investment for you. If the incentive is meaningful, you will be amazed at the cooperation that materializes and the rewards that result for you and them.

List three potential audacious goals you could pursue by yourself or with others. For each one, ask yourself: Who do I need to talk with? Call them now and make appointments to have those conversations.

NOTES

	Goal	Complete By	Next Step	Progress
Healthy				
Wealthy				
Wise				

6. Create goals you can actually achieve

If you don't have written goals you look at regularly, you don't have goals; you have a wish list. The odds of achieving goals are near zero if they aren't written down and you don't make a plan to achieve them. Your optimum goals cause you to stretch, not break.

Develop goals for the three main areas of your life: **Healthy** = exercise, physical fitness, diet, **Wealthy** = financial goals, earning goals, investments, and **Wise** = personal development, education, spiritual growth. I suggest goals that are six months to three years out. A goal just a month away is likely only part of a larger goal.

Name your goals using a verb/noun format such as issue strategic plan, draft business plan, weigh 150 pounds, or complete Alpha course. If you just write down *strategic plan*, you may forget exactly what it means. If you state *lose 10 pounds*, you may *forget* your starting weight and not know precisely when you reach your goal. Set completion dates and be specific, e.g., 5 PM on July 27, 2015, rather than *by Christmas* or *by next summer*. Goals are **how much by when**. At the appointed time, anyone should be able to see if you met your goal.

Take continuing steps to advance toward your goal. Identify actions for the next one to four weeks that will facilitate progress. Don't focus on how far away the summit is, set your sites on reaching the bridge just 200 yards ahead. As you complete each next step, take stock of your progress, it will encourage you to continue. It helps to look back to see how far you've come. Goals give your life direction.

Using the table format, list two potential goals (how much by when) for 1) Healthy, 2) Wealthy, and 3) Wise

NOTES

_____

_____

_____

_____

_____

_____

_____

_____

_____

_____

_____

_____

_____

_____

_____

_____

_____

_____

_____

_____

_____

_____

_____

_____

_____

_____

_____

_____

_____

7. Reward and celebrate

Even for small successes, celebrate achievement of goals. Promise yourself (or your team) a reward for completing key tasks, or finishing the total job. Then keep your promise and revel in your reward. Rewarding achievement helps you maintain the necessary balance in life between work and play.

Life is meant to be fun, and anyone who thinks otherwise might want to reconsider his or her outlook. Your brain needs immediate and frequent rewards to propel you forward with curiosity and interest, just like a young Labrador straining against its leash. Keeping frequent rewards on your horizon will energize you and others to move eagerly toward the next opportunity

A reward can be as simple as a walk around the building when you finish a task, 5 minutes of music after you submit a report, a complimentary lunch of sandwiches when the group hits a milestone, or a vacation to the tropics when you achieve a certain level in your savings account.

Let your team members select the milestone events they want to celebrate and the rewards to go with them.

List five small things you could celebrate with five possible rewards. Write down a major goal that you could celebrate and the reward you might use.

If you have a team, ask team members to develop possible milestone events and accompanying rewards.

NOTES

Left-to-Right Planning

Right-to-Left Planning

Top-Down Planning

8. Use the best planning approach

The three main types of planning are Left to Right, Right to Left, and Top Down. Each has its place, and each is useful in certain circumstances.

Left to right is the typical planning approach we use. We read left to right, thus, this approach is familiar. We start at the left (e.g., with a date such as now) and proceed to the right over time in days, weeks, or months. This planning approach is useful for: What do I need to do, in what order, and when will I get done?

Right to left planning starts with the end in mind (i.e., the goal, deadline, or finished product) and works back to the starting point. It is useful for: What do I need to do, in what order, and how quickly, in order to finish by the due date?

Top Down planning starts with the few key **Areas** that make up your (planning) world, then breaks down each Area into key **Activities** for each area. Next, each activity is broken down into the **Actions** needed to complete each activity. Dates are assigned to each action. A top-down approach is useful for: What all needs to be done; and which parts (activities) do I need to delete, delegate, or defer in order to be successful?

List examples for:
- *a project, goal, or endpoint where left-to-right planning would be appropriate*

- *a project, goal, or endpoint where right-to-left planning would make more sense for you*

- *a major project, e.g., a home renovation or a wedding, with multiple subprojects, goals, or endpoints where top-down planning would be a good approach.*

NOTES

9. Practice left-to-right planning

Left-to-right planning is the most common approach because left-to-right is the way most of us think and read. At the left is the starting point, e.g., now, and we proceed to the right which leads into the future. For example, you might use this planning approach in a project to build a deck.

First, draft a design, which may take two weeks to look at other decks, compare pricing on building materials, and then sketch it out. Next, take the design sketch to the city building department and get a building permit. If you haven't requested a permit before, you might want to allow 3 weeks to get the permit. Once you know what you can build, get an estimate for removing the existing landscaping, rerouting sprinklers, installing the concrete, and installing the patio roof. Allow two weeks to get estimates and select contractors. Finally, once contractors are selected, allow one week for the site prep work, one week for concrete work, and one more week to install the roof.

This planning approach helps to see what needs to be done, in what order, and verifies that it will take approximately 10 weeks based on the planning assumptions. If it's the first of May now, the project could be finished about the middle of July.

Using the example you listed in Tip 8 for left-to-right planning, sketch out the steps, the order, and the time frame for the project.

NOTES

10. Practice right-to-left planning

Again, to build a deck, what if it's the first of May now and you
want the deck in place to entertain on Father's Day (~6 weeks
away)? You can use the right-to-left method and iterate (adjust
and revise) to cut 4 weeks from the 10-week plan for a new target
of 6 weeks. For right-to-left planning, start with the end in mind.

If Father's Day is Sunday, June 17, you need all work finished by
Friday, June 15 for cleanup or an extra day for construction, if
needed. The steps are design, permitting, bid estimates, awards,
earth work, concrete work, and roof installation. If the roof is to be
done by June 15, and you allow a week (Mon - Fri) for installation,
the concrete must be installed and ready to walk on by June 11, so
it must be poured and stamped by June 4. The earth work must be
finished by June 1, so it must start on May 30. To start the earth
work by May 30, you need to award it by May 25. If you allow two
weeks for the bid- evaluation-award process, you must go out for
bid by May 14. Thus, you must have the permit approved by May
11, which means you must provide your sketched plan to the city
by May 7. To do that, you need to have the design complete by
Sunday, May 6, which gives you almost a week if you start May 1.

Because right-to-left planning identifies what must to be done to
make the end date, it may require that you take some risks you
wouldn't otherwise take if time was not a constraint. For example,
when you go out for bid on May 14, you may not have the city
permit in hand if the permitting process takes more than the week
you allowed. In this case, you take a risk in asking for bids based on
design specifications you may need to modify if the permit requires
design changes.

Using the example you listed in Tip 8 for right-to-left planning,
sketch out the steps, the order, and the time frame for the project.

NOTES

11. Practice top-down planning

Top-down planning is useful when you have a lot of things to organize, for example, if your goal were to remodel your house and get it ready for sale in one year. First, identify the four to seven key **Areas** that make up the entire scope of work required for the project. Key Areas may include 1) build a deck, 2) install an underground sprinkler system, 3) paint the home interior, 4) finish the garage interior, and 5) insulate the attic.

Next, identify four to seven key **Activities** that make up the scope of the first Area: Build the Deck. Activities may include 1) design the deck, 2) acquire a building permit, 3) bid and award the job, and 4) construct the deck. Next, break down each Activity into four to seven key **Actions**, using the verb/noun format, e.g.:

> **Design** – 1) inspect 10 neighborhood decks, 2) select construction material, 3) acquire lot plot plan, 4) draft deck footprint on lot plan, 5) stake out draft footprint, and 6) finalize the design

> **Permitting** – 1) contact the permitting agency for requirements, 2) schedule an appointment, 3) meet with the permitting person, 4) revise design, 5) submit the permit application, and 6) receive an approved permit

Break down other key Areas, until you have identified all actions needed to meet your goal. Assign dates for the activities. Review the dates, looking for peaks and valleys, and smooth them out, as needed. Each **Activity** is a mini-project that can be delegated to someone else, deferred until later, or deleted entirely.

Using the example you listed in Tip 8 for top-down planning, sketch out the steps, the order, and the time frame for the project. Which mini-projects (i.e., Activities) lend themselves to delegation, deferral, or deletion?

NOTES

12. Establish a schedule and work to it

Once you have identified all required activities, the next step is schedule sequencing, i.e., planning the sequence and timing of activities needed to complete the project. There are mandatory (hard logic) constraints to schedule sequencing, e.g., you have to put up the walls before you paint them. There also are discretionary (soft logic) constraints, i.e., your preferences for the order of activities. For example, you might prefer to paint the walls before you lay the carpet. However, if the painters aren't available when you need them, you could install the carpet first, and then protect the carpet when you paint the walls later.

Once you have established a schedule and are working to it, don't lose sight of the soft logic (preferences) that are built in. These are opportunities for change that you may need in the future to make up time. To "fast track" a project, you can conduct some activities in parallel rather than in a series of steps. For example, you may initially plan to complete the design before you start construction. However, when the design is delayed, you could start construction (e.g., prepare the site and install the underground utilities) while you are still finishing the design. You may take more risks in fast tracking, but it could be worth it. Evaluate the risks against the rewards.

Remember, your initial plan is your preferred sequence for getting things done, but it's not necessarily how it MUST be done.

Think about something you are doing now with an established order (sequence). Does it have to be done in that sequence? If you want to gain some time or complete it sooner, what could you do out of sequence? What would the risks be?

NOTES

_____

_____

_____

_____

_____

_____

_____

_____

_____

_____

_____

_____

_____

_____

_____

_____

_____

_____

_____

_____

_____

_____

_____

_____

_____

_____

_____

13. Plan your week and plan your day

At the beginning of each week, set aside 15 minutes to plan the week. Make sure you plug in recreational and social activities along with appointments and time to work on important tasks. Add more detail; plug in essential things you want to accomplish each day. Be realistic; plan for interruptions and leave blocks open for unanticipated but important things that might come up.

Every morning, use the first 10 minutes to organize your thoughts, plan your day, and prioritize your actions. Identify the three to five things that you could get done that day to move the needle toward meeting your important goals. Spend time on important things, not urgent things. (Tip 24 explains important vs. urgent.) Don't let yourself open e-mail, make phone calls, read the paper, or engage in other distractions until you've planned your day and decided when you're going to do those things and how much time you are willing to allocate to them. Don't schedule back-to-back activities all day long. That's just not realistic, and you'll set yourself up for failure.

If you haven't planned out today, stop and plan it right now. If it's nearly over, plan tomorrow. Leave yourself a reminder for tomorrow to plan your day before you start anything. It could be a "note to self" in your planner if you look at that first thing, or it could be a sticky note posted on the kitchen cabinet or your bathroom mirror.

NOTES

14. Make it a habit

A few years ago NASA conducted an experiment to study the long-term effects of disorientation on the human brain, mind and body. Test subjects wore goggles with convex lenses that turned everything in view upside-down! They wore the goggles for several weeks during all normal activities, e.g., eating, reading, working, while perceiving everything upside-down. NASA wanted to know if the disorientation would cause nausea, high blood-pressure, or other ill effects. However, after three to four weeks something startling and amazing happened! One by one, the subjects, while still wearing the upside-down goggles, started to see things right-side-up. Their brains were rewiring and adjusting to the view. The experiment demonstrated that if you do something continuously, without a break, for approximately 30 days, your brain lays down new pathways so the activity becomes "normal."

You can turn good practices into habits by following the lesson of the NASA experiment. Make a list of daily habits you want to acquire and then perform them each day, checking them off your list. Desired habits can grow from small things, like meditating for 5 minutes, exercising for 15 minutes, sitting in gratitude and thankfulness for 5 minutes, planning your day, reaching out to friends or clients, or engaging in other things of importance to you. The key is to start with a list that helps you remember to do them each day. Eventually your activity will become a normal practice or habit, and you won't need to remind yourself to do it.

Write down five things you will start doing or tracking on a daily basis to establish desired habits. Make up a 30-day list of these items so you can check them off each day for a month.

NOTES

15. Revise your plan

The only thing certain about a great plan is that it will change. Goals or end results should not be changed lightly, but even the best plans seldom are executed as planned from start to finish. Be willing to adjust your plan based on lessons learned, new developments, new information, and/or ideas and feedback from others.

Successful people make decisions quickly (in a timely fashion) and change their minds very slowly. So don't change the plan every time you encounter a bump in the road, but think about it. Make thoughtful decisions. The primary caution is to avoid getting so enamored with your plan that you are reluctant to change it. Often, when people put a lot of effort into developing a great plan, they aren't willing to listen to other or better ideas because *that's calling my baby ugly.*

Did you ever start painting a room and it just didn't look good? Did you keep painting because that was the plan or did you stop and start over with a new color? Revising your plan for the right reason can be a means to success.

Think back to a time when revising a plan earlier could have helped you accomplish a goal more effectively. Write down an example in which holding onto the goal but revising the plan ultimately would have been more effective.

NOTES

16. Identify the next steps

When developing goals, always identify the next step you can take within one to four weeks. If you have the next step identified, you don't have to rethink it each day or decide what to do; you already have it figured out. When your goal is several months or years away, it's easy to put off working on it. *I'll just start tomorrow.* You need the next step clearly in front of you to keep you going.

Once, I had a goal to complete the Toast Masters Competent Communicator program, which entailed giving a series of 10 speeches in 6 months. My next steps always included things like: *draft speech #2 by the end of next week (one week out) and deliver it within the next two weeks (two weeks out)* OR *draft speeches #3 and #4 within the next two weeks (two weeks out) and deliver speech #3 within the next four weeks (four weeks out).* It's much easier to get your head around short- and near-term actions, and it's easier to put them on your action list when they need to be done soon.

Review the goals you drafted in Tip 6. Identify two to three things for each goal that can be done in the next one to four weeks to move you closer to your goal. Assign a date for taking each action and schedule time to work on it, using your planner, calendar, iPhone, or whatever system you use. Don't read another word or do anything else until you've completed this task.

NOTES

17. Practice the Rule of 5

One of my mentors, Jack Canfield, teaches the Rule of 5, and I've used it successfully in many areas to complete big and small goals. The premise is that if you walked up to the biggest oak tree in the forest and took FIVE swings at it each day with a sharp axe, eventually it would come down. The same can be said about taking small but regular steps toward any goal. Take five small steps toward your goal every day and you will get there.

For example, your small steps may be making phone calls, sending e-mails, writing a paragraph, sending a postcard, looking up a fact, ordering a book, watching an instructional video, reading two pages, or doing 10 pushups.

Once, I led an effort to coordinate a public event where the host organization wanted 100 paying customers to attend. I asked the planning team to employ the Rule of 5. Each day, each team member did five small things that would push us toward our goal of putting on a quality event with the desired attendance. Their small actions included calling and inviting a person, sending two e-mail invitations, posting two fliers, etc. With a team of six people taking actions five days per week for two months, the planning team undertook over 1,200 individual actions to drive us toward a successful event! It is a powerful strategy.

Pick one of your goals or something else you want to achieve. Make a list of 10 to 15 small things you could do to move you toward that goal. Each day, complete five of those actions. You will be amazed at how much more you get done and how much faster (and more often) you realize your goals with the Rule of 5.

NOTES

18. Take action and keep moving

Nothing happens until you take action. Planning, organizing, and strategizing have their place, but without action, nothing gets done. Napoleon Hill, author of the classic book, *Think and Grow Rich,* said, *"...knowledge is useless unless you make a specific plan, for purpose, to accomplish an objective..."* In other words, unless you act on your knowledge, it is of little value. Knowing how to effectively raise funds for a non-profit organization is useless until you put that knowledge to work and raise the funds (i.e., take action).

As you take action, you may need to acquire and use feedback in order to sustain your momentum. As long as you are moving, collecting feedback, making any necessary course adjustments, and continuing the action, you can advance productively toward your goal. Piloting an airplane or a ship requires continual course adjustments during the trip. As long as It's moving forward and being redirected toward its destination, ultimately it will get there. If the plane sat on the ground or the ship waited in the harbor until a perfect plan were in place to maintain a perfect course, it never would leave and thus never get to its destination. You have to take action, be willing to accept and use feedback, and make corrections along the way in order to maintain progress.

What have you been planning or thinking about that you haven't accomplished yet because you're not ready to take action? What is one action you can take in the next 24 hours that will start you down the path toward your goal? What are three more actions you can take within the next five days that will move you farther down the road?

NOTES

19. Use the next 15 minutes

What can you accomplishment in the next 15 minutes? This is a great question to ask yourself several times a day, especially in the afternoon when you're losing focus and enthusiasm.

In just 15 minutes you can take several small actions that will really move you toward your goal. They might be • calling 3 banks to get rates for their credit card processing programs • calling the university advisor and making an appointment to discuss re-enrolling • sending two e-mails asking for help on a project • calling people you respect and asking them if they will be your mentor for six months • inviting someone to lunch so you can ask for advice on a perplexing topic • putting an ad on Craig's List to get rid of the snow tires you don't need • calling the fitness center to make an appointment with the personal trainer • finding the nearest person to brainstorm ideas for solving a problem.

Take 15 minutes right now to complete as many things as possible that will move you toward a goal. It's okay if they are small steps, as long as they move you forward.

NOTES

20. Use the 30-minute blitz

The 30-minute blitz is another strategy for helping you accomplish
your goals. Set the timer for 30 minutes then go crazy getting
things done until the timer stops. Whip yourself into a frenzy with
100% focus, no distractions, no answering the phone, no petting
the cat, no looking at your email, no texting – just 30 minutes of
unabashed, all-out effort toward your area of focus.

You might apply this to cleaning your office, for example. If you
just went crazy for 30 minutes at full-out speed, throwing things
away, putting things away, wiping down surfaces, emptying boxes,
filling boxes for storage, recycling binders and shredding, you could
make enormous strides toward a clean, organized office. The blitz
approach is ideal for something you may have been putting off for
months because it's a lot of work, not fun, or *you never have
the time.*

Often, when we look at procrastinated projects, like cleaning your
garage, we envision a half-day effort. Because we never have a
spare half day, it just doesn't get done. However, we can do just
about anything for 30 minutes, especially if we make it a game,
charging full-speed ahead in an all-out frenzy to get things done.
Usually, you will find that a 30-minute blitz can complete half of
that 4-hour job. Making just one more 30-minute blitz in a couple
of days could finish the task.

*List the activity or area of focus that could most use a 30-minute
blitz. When will you dedicate the 30 minutes? Schedule the blitz.*

NOTES

21. Partner for accountability

Using an accountability partner is an ideal way to drive super achievement. Two partners hold each other accountable for completing things they committed to complete. It works best in a face-to-face situation, for example, for workers in nearby offices. However, it can be conducted by phone, email or texting, as well.

Partner A declares three to five actions he or she will take or the tasks that will be completed before the partners' next contact (e.g., tomorrow morning at 8 AM). Partner B acknowledges and records Partner A's commitment and declares his or her own commitment for accomplishing three to five things by the next contact. Partner A acknowledges and records Partner B's commitment. At the next contact, Partner A reports on his/her progress and identifies actions he or she will complete before the next contact. Partner B records the commitment and makes his or her commitments, which Partner A records. The discussion entails only the partners' reports and new commitments. There is no explaining, blaming, or brow beating. If something didn't get done, the only question is: *Are you willing to recommit to the action?*

This approach works best if you dedicate five minutes to it each day, Monday through Friday, or three days a week. The purpose is to keep you moving forward. When time nears for the appointed call, it's amazing what you'll do to complete your assignment so you don't have to report you didn't do it.

List three people who are potential accountability partners. Write down a date by which you'll talk with them to make an Accountability Partner agreement. Write down the date you will begin to use the strategy. Commit to using this strategy in partnership with each other for two months. At the end of two months, evaluate your success. Recommit with your partner for another period or find another Partner, if needed.

NOTES

22. Make it a project

The beauty of a project is that it accomplishes something or provides a product or service within a time period bound by a starting point and an end point. Nearly all things can be *projectized,* i.e., achieved by making them projects.

For example, you can projectize becoming a better speaker by creating the actions and defining the endpoint. The project might include completing the Toast Masters Competent Communicator series of 10 speeches by a certain date. Similarly, you can projectize becoming a better golfer. The golf improvement project might entail taking six group lessons and two private lessons, hitting 1,000 range balls, and playing 72 holes of golf by a certain date. (Note that this is a process goal, not a milestone goal.)

Projectizing establishes an end date, so you increase your probability of completing the project and achieving your goal. With a project, you can complete it, celebrate it, and move on. If you start down the path of becoming a better speaker without defined actions and an endpoint, you may never be as good as you could be. There's no sense of accomplishment, and you don't get to move on to other things. Frequently we get tired of it because we don't see the progress or gain a sense of accomplishment. Then we quit, which is demoralizing. By setting an endpoint, you can achieve and recognize your progress; and when you reach your goal, you can free up that block of time for another important priority or take the initial priority to the next level.

List three things you are working on now that could be projectized. Define completion and establish end dates.

NOTES

23. Prioritize outcomes not actions

Prioritizing project outcomes increases your odds of actually completing the project and achieving your goal. It's important to prioritize the *outcomes* rather than the *actions*. While this may sound like splitting hairs, it really is an important distinction.

In the examples (from Tip 22), actions for becoming a better golfer, included hitting range balls and playing several rounds of golf. The actions for becoming a better speaker included attending Toastmaster meetings, preparing speeches, and delivering speeches. If you were to compare and prioritize the actions for playing nine holes of golf Monday night versus attending a Toastmaster meeting, the round of golf might very well come out on top (I know I could come up with many reasons to support that prioritization).

However, if you prioritized outcomes – becoming a better golfer or becoming a better speaker – you might come up with a different order of priority. Becoming a better speaker might be a higher priority because it will serve your future in more important ways than becoming a better golfer.

Review the three things you projectized in Tip 22 and compare and prioritize individual actions. Then compare and prioritize the outcomes of each project. List three other projects and, for each, compare and prioritize outcomes rather than the actions.

NOTES

24. Test the 80/20 principle

Pareto, an economist who lived over a hundred years ago, developed the 80/20 Principle by studying cause and effect. He noted that 80% of the effects came from 20% of the causes. Initially, he was looking at land ownership versus population (80% of the land was owned by 20% of the people). Then, he observed that 80% of the peas in his garden came from 20% of the pods.

As it turns out, we can apply this principle to almost everything! In your relationships, 80% of your happiness and fulfillment comes from 20% of your contacts. Now, it might not be exactly 80/20, but the principle is the same. Look at your to-do list for the day and identify 20% of the items on your list that actually result in 80% of the progress toward your important goals. The trick to prioritizing is to isolate and identify the 20% that has the greatest value to you. Once identified, prioritize your time to concentrate work on items with the greatest potential reward. Do more higher-value activities and fewer lower-value activities!

Sometimes we let our to-do lists get full of things that seem urgent (like returning a DVD to Red Box), but in the scheme of things, actually they are not really important. As Timothy Ferris, author of *The 4-Hour Work Week* points out, *"If the day ended and either you wrote the first two pages of your new book or you returned the DVD on time and avoided a $1 charge, which would have been more important?"* Which really would have moved you closer to your goal?

Look at your to-do list and identify the 20% (one out of every five items) that actually will move you toward your goals. Schedule time now and in the next week to work on high-value activities.

NOTES

Q1 – Important and Urgent

Q2 – Important but Not Urgent

Q3 – Not Important but Urgent

Q4 – Not Important and Not Urgent

25. Test with the ABCs of prioritization

Eisenhower and
Stephen Covey
used the Four-
Quadrant Process
for prioritizing, i.e.,
sorting out what's

Prioritize Your Actions		
	Urgent	Not Urgent
Important	Q1 (Priority A)	Q2 (Priority B)
Not Important	Q3 (Priority C)	Q4 (Priority D)

important and urgent. Quadrant 1 (Q1) is both important and
urgent. Quadrant 2 (Q) is important, but not urgent. Quadrant 3
(Q3) is not important but is urgent. Quadrant 4 (Q4) is not
important and not urgent.

Priority A items in Q1 are important and need action now, e.g., the
crying baby, the fire in the waste basket, some phone calls, and
what the boss needs for his noon meeting.

Priorlty B items in Q2 are very important, but you have time to
work on them, e.g., exercise and diet, your vocation, planning
activities, and continuing education.

Priority C items in Q3 aren't really important, but they may appear
urgent, e.g., interruptions, distractions, many phone calls, and
most emails or text messages.

Priority D items in Q4 are not important and not urgent. We
usually know when we are engaged in these activities. Examples
are: trivia, time wasters, busy work, and things others could do.

Minimize Q1 (fire drills) by maximizing Q2 (preventive action).
Routinely taking care of your teeth will minimize unplanned dental
emergencies. Focus on Priority B activities daily. You never
eliminate all Priority A items, but working on Priority B items gives
you more control. Schedule Priority C items in blocks, e.g., 30-
minute blocks. Do not put any Q4 items on your schedule.

For each quadrant, list four to seven actions. Put some of the
Priority B items into your daily and weekly schedule now.

NOTES

26. Know what you need to complete today

Every day, decide on the top one, two or three things you will complete before going to bed. They don't need to be major, but they should be things that move you toward your objectives. For example, you may decide in the morning that you will invite three people to your company's open house next month because it's essential for your business to have a good turnout. Mark it on your calendar as a SNUD (sleep not until done) and complete the invitations, even if it is 10:30 PM.

It's too easy at the end of the day to say: *I didn't get as far as I wanted, so I'll just send out six invitations tomorrow.* It's likely you don't always complete everything on your daily schedule. If you do, raise the bar for yourself! However, we need to identify those critical few things that will keep us moving forward, and we need to hold ourselves accountable for knocking them out.

Often, the reason some things don't get done is that they may not be urgent. However, they are likely very important. For example, you might decide that you are going to buy a thank you card today so tomorrow you can give it to the administrative person who really went above and beyond. It's something you might not otherwise get around to doing. It's easy to assume you'll do it tomorrow, but then tomorrow comes and you're busy so, once again, you decide you'll just do something nice for her next time. Ultimately, your good intention never plays out.

List one to three things that you will complete before going to bed tonight.

NOTES

27. Delete, delegate, and defer

Whether it's emails, actions, projects, or friends, there are three things you can do to simplify your life – delete, delegate and defer. Ask yourself if you really need to look at a particular Facebook post, the email from an association in which you'd really rather not participate, or another bad joke from a friend. The more that you can say *"no,"* the better off you will be. Just delete them and keep going. If it's something that really needs attention, can it be done by someone else? Can you hand it to someone who is better equipped to address it? If you need to take care of it, do you have to do it now or can it be deferred until next week or next month? Just because they want your comments by tomorrow, doesn't mean you always give those comments by tomorrow.

When you conducted your Top-Down Planning exercise in Tip 11, it may have felt overwhelming to identify the dozens of things to do. The good news is that, through the exercises, you were able to clarify what is required to complete your goals, which provides an ideal opportunity for prioritizing activities. You can delete activities you can do without, delegate any activities you can, and defer activities you don't need to do right now.

Go back and look at the exercise in Tip 11. Which activities can be deleted? Which activities can be delegated? To whom can you delegate them, and by when will you have them delegated? Which activities actually don't have to be done in the time period you planned? For how long can they be deferred without impacting achievement of your goals?

NOTES

28. Be effective versus efficient

We want to feel productive and effective. Our natural tendency is to very efficiently work so we can check off a bunch of to-dos. However, efficiently doing unimportant things doesn't make us effective, and it doesn't advance us in meeting our goals.

Effectiveness is getting the right things done; completing things that really move the needle toward accomplishment on the projects that are very important. You are effective when you demonstrate the ability to focus efforts on actions that matter.

Efficiency, on the other hand, is doing something quickly and correctly, like zooming through your e-mail eight times a day and quickly sorting the things to delete, delegate, defer, and do now. But the real question is: Did the three hours spent in your mailbox really move you closer to achieving your key objective: to buy a piece of commercial property, to complete and turn in your class project, or to submit your proposal? Did it get you closer to developing that new product you want to offer for sale on your website? In one of Peter Drucker's books, he points out, *"there are few things less pleasing to the Lord, and less productive, than an engineering department that rapidly turns out beautiful blueprints for the wrong product."* Thus, being efficient is rapidly turning out things. Being effective is *turning out the right things - rapidly.*

List 3 things you do very efficiently that aren't really the most effective use of your time. Describe what you will do to cut in half the time you spend doing these things.

NOTES

29. Block out times

One of the most important things you can do to increase your effectiveness is to block out periods on your calendar to work on your top-priority actions. Schedule an hour Tuesday morning to work on XX and an hour Thursday morning to work on YY. Decide ahead of time whether you will allow anything to bump them and cause you to reschedule; if not, everything else will have to wait.

During the scheduled blocks of time, go full out with no distractions. Hit the restroom before you start and fill your coffee cup, if that's your vice. Turn off the e-mail "ding," and turn off your phone ringer. Think back a month ago. What if you had started then? What could you have accomplished by spending an additional eight hours, dedicated, focused, and in high gear, working on your top priority?

Identify the one priority to which you will dedicate two hours a week for the next month working with intentional focus?

Right now, schedule two hours each week, noting specific dates and times for your priority work.

What might come up that could preempt your important work? List the few, if any, things that might emerge and cause you to reschedule.

If anything does occur that causes you to reschedule, immediately schedule a new time for your priority activity. Don't let it fall by the wayside.

NOTES

30. Avoid email

Email is like a chronic illness. Over time it can sap your strength, drain you of your passion, and become all you think about. To some, it is a badge of honor. *"I got 232 emails yesterday; I'm just drowning!"* To which the response is invariably, *"Oh yeah? I was on vacation for three days and when I got back I had 727 new emails in my inbox!!"* The first person never had a chance at winning the *I am so in demand* competition.

No matter how deftly you go through your email, deleting some, delegating others, deferring a few, and *doing now* those things that make the cut, at the end of the day you still have to ask: *Did the three hours spent on email really move you toward your goal of getting the new contract out for bid – or whatever your most important objective was?* Being effective is much more important than being efficient.

To maximize your effectiveness, set times and time limits for email. For example, you may decide that you aren't going to look at email until you've planned your day and completed one task. If you start your day at 6:00 AM, you can use the first 30 minutes for planning and working on the scheduled task. At 6:30 you can check your email. Give yourself a time limit, e.g., only 15 minutes for cleaning it out and making short replies, as appropriate. If something warrants a longer reply, schedule and prioritize it with the other things on your to-do list. Make that reply only when it's scheduled and only spend the time you have allocated.

Establish a daily schedule for email, for example, 10 minutes at 10:00 AM, 1:00 PM, 4:00 PM, and 7:00 PM. Reschedule and prioritize anything that will cause you to exceed the allotted 10 minutes.

NOTES

31. Write it down

Writing down the things we need to do is easy and reasonable. Then, why don't we do it routinely? We assume our powerful brains will store that information until we need it. And of course they do. However, frequently the recall function of our brains isn't as good as the storage part of our brains. We haven't properly set up the indexing system or the recall triggers that help us effectively associate needed actions with other information.

Although there are ways to improve our recall functions, the simplest and most reliable way to remember things is to write down everything in a place and in a way that comes back into your consciousness at the right time. You could use a day planner where you record key conversations, commitments made by others, facts you learned, etc. With a planner, you can go back and review your notations any time. You can use it to write down every new action or commitment you make. If you agree to draft a white paper for Paula by next Friday, write down the action for today or tomorrow so you can prioritize it on your to-do list. Also, make an entry on next Friday: *White paper for Paula due today.* It only takes a couple of times to "space out" and forget something before you are known as someone who cannot be trusted to deliver as promised. Getting into the habit of writing things down can help you be successful.

What system do you use (or will you start using) to record new information, ideas, facts acquired, actions to take, commitments made, and appointments to keep? It could be a day planner, logbook, journal, smart phone, or your Outlook calendar on your computer. Identify ten things you have been thinking about doing. Write them down for practice and improve the likelihood of completing them on time.

NOTES

32. Outsource for $10

Don't do anything you can outsource for babysitter wages. Make a very long list of all the things that could be done by someone like a high school student or near minimum-wage handy-person. Examples include filing, cleaning the garage, washing windows, organizing the library, setting up an external hard drive, backing up your files, entering contact information into your data base from all the business cards you've collected, or cutting back the roses.

This effectiveness approach applies to the office setting too. Ask yourself what you are doing that could be done by administrative or other assistance. Typically, we tell ourselves: *I have to do this; no one else will do it just the way I want or need it done.* When you hear yourself say that, reconsider how absurd that is. Your job is to delegate fully and clearly, establishing the touch points (i.e., when you will check on it to ensure it is meeting your needs), so you can engage In more important matters.

There is a reason the CEO of the company doesn't make her own travel arrangements. She could, but it isn't the best use of her time. She won't be CEO for long if she is making travel arrangements and justifying her efforts by saying, *"Our secretary doesn't know when I like to travel, what seats I like, the layovers I'll tolerate, how early I like to arrive in a city."*

Figure out when to outsource and how to delegate clearly and with the right touch points. Stop yourself whenever you hear yourself say: *it's easier for me to do it than to train someone else to do it.* That attitude is an indicator you are being ineffective.

List seven things you will outsource or delegate to someone else.

NOTES

33. Be intentional

Never go into a meeting, to a job site, or to an event without a purpose. Think about it ahead of time and determine what you want to give, get, or accomplish. What would success look like at the end of the meeting or event? Do you want to plant the seed of a new idea, get a commitment, reach an agreement, get names, meet a specific person, or gain information?

Without a pre-determined purpose, you won't know whether it was successful or not. For example, you may want to build up the confidence of a subordinate or teammate and your thoughtful plan is to use the meeting to commend your teammate in front of the right audience. You may want to evaluate the participation of another attendee for a future hiring decision or determine whether the person running the meeting has the skills you need to lead a future project review for you.

At events, decide who (or what kind of person) you want to meet, and make a plan to accomplish it. Ask to be introduced to a specific person or ask the event organizer to introduce you to the type person you want to meet. Never sit at an empty table because you don't control who will come and sit with you. Always arrive early, greet people coming in, watch for the person or type of person you want to meet, and then join his or her table. Never leave it to chance.

What event or situation will you be going into in the next 48 hours (maybe a family gathering, volunteer group meeting, or work situation)? What intention can you identify ahead of time? What do you need to think through or jot down to prepare for the opportunity?

NOTES

34. Say no

No is such a small word – and yet it is so hard to say. Focusing on your goals can help you say no. Blocking time for important, but often not scheduled priorities such as family and friends, also can help. First, reinforce for yourself that you and your priorities are important — that seems to be the hardest part in learning to say no. Once convinced of their importance, it gets easier to say no to unimportant things.

What can you decline to do? Your involvement may have started a while ago because it served your purpose then or you thought you *should* help out. Ask yourself why you are still involved and how it fits with your priorities. To ease away from it, you can give one cycle notice, e.g., *I'll take the meeting minutes one more time but then you'll need to find someone else.*

Be ruthless about saying no to requests that aren't an effective use of your skills, time, or energy. Just because you *can* do something doesn't mean you *should*.

Say yes to things you really want to do. If you spend your time doing things you *should* and never what you *could*, your mind will rebel, you'll lose your focus, and you'll build resentments.

List the three things you will decline and make arrangements to stop doing them.

NOTES

35. Commit, don't overcommit

I'm sure you've heard someone say, *I'm over committed!* Actually, they are saying they are *not committed.* If you are committed to improving your marketability and getting your Project Management Professional (PMP) certification, then you do what is required to achieve your goals. You study, you take classes, you study some more, you complete the laborious application, and you take the exam until you pass it.

I've had people attend my PMP Exam Preparation Boot Camp classes then later say they haven't taken the exam because they are over committed. Their excuse is they have too many things going on. In reality, they have a commitment problem, and it's not over commitment. They aren't committed to a few priority things and doing what it takes to complete them. Instead, they are committing their time to many unimportant things, and they are not giving any of them the attention needed to be successful. When you hear yourself or others talk about being overcommitted, recognize that actually you are *not committed* and may have lost sight of your priorities.

What are you NOT doing very well because you feel overcommitted? List all competing activities that "prevent" you from doing important things well and then prioritize your activities. In order to be successful in the areas most important to you, list the lower-priority activities you are going to eliminate, i.e., delegate or delete.

NOTES

36. Assume you are responsible

Assume you are responsible for everything. It's not true, but do it anyway. How differently would you review a procedure if YOU, rather than the procedure's author or performer, were responsible for its success? How differently would the clerk at the hardware store treat you if he or she assumed responsibility for the store's success?

When we take responsibility for outcomes, we automatically accelerate our game. We see things from a higher level than when we perceived *it was someone else's responsibility.* Even if it's difficult to understand how you are responsible, take responsibility for your response to events. If your team is late in delivering essential supplies to a customer, don't dismiss it by saying you did YOUR part, others made it late. That attitude doesn't help the project or customer relations, which can impact whether your team gets future projects. Take responsibility by asking, *"If I were responsible, how could I learn from what happened? What will I do differently next time to ensure delivery is on time?"*

If everyone on the team takes responsibility to make it better, regardless of who actually dropped the ball on delivery, the end result will be incredibly better. No one wins when everyone points fingers at someone else and claiming, *it's not my fault.* The change in attitude and taking responsibility should start with you.

List three things or outcomes you will start acting on as if you were responsible. What actions are you going to take for each one? Where and when can you make it clear to others that you are stepping up to influence the outcomes? Note: the purpose is to set a good example, not play the martyr. If you find yourself seeking sympathy or a pat on the head, you've missed the point.

NOTES

37. Ask for feedback

The most useful thing you can do to improve as a leader, employee, or person is to ask for feedback and take action as warranted. Everyone else already knows; why wouldn't you want to know? Frequently, people are afraid of hurting your feelings. They may believe you don't want unsolicited feedback, or they don't want to make waves. You have to ask for feedback, thank the person for giving it, and then act on it if it will help you be more effective.

Invite someone to your next status meeting, safety meeting, or speaking engagement for the express purpose of giving you feedback afterward. Select someone you respect who will give you honest, useful feedback. Ask him or her to evaluate facial expressions of the audience or body language you may miss.

Once I sat in on a client's workshop and observed that my client's response to one attendee caused that person to shut down and stop participating for the next 20 minutes. It was a just a miscommunication. However, because my client was focused on the entire audience and the topic at hand, he wasn't aware of the attendee and didn't realize what he'd done (and it turns out he did it more than once). Fortunately, my client asked for feedback and then used the information to make a simple correction, which helped improve his bottom line for years to come. If he hadn't asked for feedback, he never would have known why some people were being alienated.

What is the next opportunity you have to ask for feedback? Who will you ask? By when will you ask?

NOTES

38. Assume authority and empower yourself

No doubt you've heard people say, *I can't do that,* or *they won't let me do that,* or *I don't know if I'm allowed to do that.*

Yet others say things like, *I don't know how, but I'll find out...* or *I've never been told not to,* or *the worst that can happen is someone will tell me no.* Empowerment is much less official than we think. The best employees and bosses are the ones who take the bull by the horns and go figure it out. They assume they can do it and just do what it takes. The phrase, *"Better to ask for forgiveness, than to seek approval,"* actually applies 98% of the time. For the very few times when it is the wrong choice – oh, well – don't take it personally.

It is a winner's mindset to believe you can do anything, or will go down in flames trying. I once had a great boss who sometimes allowed the lines between subordinate roles to blur. It was interesting to watch those who would step up and take the lead or responsibility for tasks and others who would hold back and let others usurp control. I observed three types of people: 1) people who waited to be told what they should do, 2) people who took advantage of others for personal gain, and 3) people who stepped up to lead and shared credit, as appropriate.

Write down three areas or activities where you could assume you have more authority.

NOTES

39. Make others successful

The best way to ensure your success – at work and in life – is to make others successful first. The old phrase, *"Ask and you shall receive,"* has been replaced with, *"Give and you shall receive."* The more you give to others, and the more effort you make to help others, the more it comes back to you.

Look for ways to give back to your mentors – even little nuggets of information, job notices (not just for them but for other protégés), or leads on opportunities. Nobody likes to give, give, give; so don't expect it of others. Instead, be the one who gives – to peers, subordinates, and bosses. Help them out, offer to assist, look something up, give them a resource, send them a link, give them the contact information of the person who detailed your car, or point them to the web designer you found.

Too many people look at the world as a zero sum game rather than as an abundant world. That is, if you get something there must be less for the rest of us. There is enough success for everyone. I've helped people find a free service; and years later, I've received a profitable speaking contract from them. You don't help people expecting something in return. You do it because it is the right thing to do. Over time, others want to help you, too.

Some people will never return the favor and that's fine. They're just not there yet. Maybe they haven't had the opportunity or they just don't get it. But that's okay. Giving has its own rewards.

List at least three people for whom you would like to do something within the next week. Write down at least six potential things you could do for them in the next week. Now put those actions into your planner or scheduling system so you will do them.

NOTES

40. Measure it

Many people have said if you can't measure it, it's not important or worth doing. Although there may be exceptions, it is largely true. If it really is important, you should be able to measure progress or establish some meaningful metrics (how much by when).

You get what you measure, so always measure what you want, not what you don't want. For example, if you want to improve customer satisfaction, measure the numbers of times they're satisfied (e.g., current customer satisfaction rates are 97%, and the target is 99%). Don't measure dissatisfaction levels (e.g., currently at 3%, the target is to drive dissatisfaction down to 1%). You achieve where you place your energy and focus. If you focus on dissatisfaction, too often that's what you'll get.

When it's difficult to measure, ask: *What would success look like?* For example, if your goal is to be more thoughtful and to do a better job in recognizing your staff, ask: *What would it look like if I were doing it well?* That vision of success can help you devise measureable actions, for example, at least three times a week I will personally extend a sincere thank you to someone for his or her contribution to our activity. Furthermore, at least once a week I'll send a note to persons outside my organization with my thanks for their contributions. Or, if your goal is maintaining customer satisfaction at a level of 8 or above on a scale of 1 to 10, you can survey customers by developing questions and asking them to rank your performance each month.

Identify one thing you are doing now that is important but that you are not measuring or trending. Develop two metrics you could use (how much by when) to measure and track it.

NOTES

41. Hold a daily coordination call

The daily coordination call is an excellent tool I learned about from Marie, a good friend and fellow project manager. We were running a fast-track project, and time was critical. There was no time to let something languish a day or two, or worse yet, to find out at the weekly status meeting something was delayed three days ago and we missed the opportunity to influence it.

In our case, we had a 15-minute phone call that was hard-scheduled each morning with approximately six key project contributors. We followed a standard agenda, and we all recorded our own notes. The field persons reported on subprojects, giving a quick status on tasks completed yesterday, scheduled for today, and planned for tomorrow. They identified any issues, any help needed, and whose help they needed. The issues weren't solved during the call, but participants agreed on the follow-up actions, schedule and deadlines. The engineering lead discussed a summary of design changes, estimated turnaround times, and design changes released since the last call. Everyone had an opportunity to discuss the need for any changes or actions to be reprioritized or delayed.

The purpose was to 1) determine if we had completed what we had planned to complete 2) identify what are were doing today, and 3) provide a heads-up for activities we were planning for tomorrow. The daily coordination call didn't take the place of longer-term planning and scheduling meetings, but it kept things moving and facilitated near real-time resolution of issues as they materialized.

What activities or projects in your work or personal life would benefit from a short coordination call each day (or other timely frequency)?

NOTES

42. Delegate fully

Delegating is a skill that few people have developed well. Yet, most of us think we do it *really* well. The problem is often we don't want to let go of things (all the way). We delegate the task but hold onto the reigns because we don't want to give up control or we think we can't live with the consequences if things don't turn out well.

Delegating does not mean relinquishing control; it actually means *establishing* control. Typically, when we delegate, the other party views us as micro-managing if we follow up with them. That's because we didn't establish the right *touch points* up front. For example, to fill a new supervisor position in your organization, you could delegate the hiring task to a manager reporting to you.

You may need assurance of the candidate's suitability. Thus, when you delegate, establish key *touch points*, clarifying where and how you want to be involved. Tell the hiring manager you'd like a briefing on the short list of candidates and another briefing on the selection process when the finalists are selected.

By establishing touch points for your involvement up front, the hiring manager knows his or her responsibilities and your expectations for involvement. You both know what is delegated and what is held back. This clear understanding minimizes your being viewed as micro-managing.

Think back on a delegation activity that did not go as well as you would have liked (either as the delegator or delegate). What touch points could have been established at the beginning of the delegation? How could that different approach have changed the participants' feelings about the process and the outcome?

NOTES

43. Build in contingency

Build smart contingency into everything you do. *How much contingency depends on the consequence of failure.* If you're meeting friends across town for dinner, the impact of being five minutes late is low. If you are interviewing for an incredible job opportunity, however, the impact of showing up five minutes late is much higher.

In everything you do, think about the consequence of failure (or a poor outcome), and build in contingency to fit the situation. My local newspaper reported the story of a group of girls missing a plane to Mexico for their spring break; such a sad story. It took longer than they expected to get to the airport because traffic was worse than normal. What was the consequence? They missed about a day and a half of their Mexican spring break, and it cost (their parents) several hundreds if not thousands of dollars in additional airfare to put them on a different flight. It was the perfect opportunity for the girls to learn the value of building in contingency in order to avoid a bad outcome.

What is one activity you have now or coming up that could benefit from contingency planning? What could go wrong? What could impact or prevent your desired outcome? List three contingencies you could put in place to 1) avoid the risk of a poor outcome, 2) mitigate the risk (make it less likely to happen or not as bad if it does happen), or 3) spread/share the risk with others.

NOTES

44. Define an exit strategy

Develop an exit strategy before you agree to a new commitment. Too often as we add more and more activities to our busy lives, eventually we find we truly are overcommitted or engaged in activities for which our passion has diminished.

When you are asked to volunteer, join a group, or take on a new role, determine your exit strategy up front. It may be as simple as stating, *"I will help out until August 31."* When August 31 comes around, you are automatically excused with no explanation required, no surprises, and no hurt feelings. Of course, if you choose at that point to extend your help until December 31, you are free to do so. Again, you have an exit strategy, and no one will be surprised when your support or involvement ceases at the end of December. An abrupt exit, on the other hand, can leave people thinking you quit because something upset you. They may even worry it was something they did or said.

A pre-determined exit strategy also can be useful to the overall cause. When people understand your support to the group is limited, and not just an open-ended use of your time, they have an incentive to make the group and its activities as productive as possible in order to take advantage of your expertise while it's available. The drive for effectiveness and productivity actually makes the activity more rewarding for all participants.

What is one thing you are doing or contemplating for which you should develop an exit strategy? What is your strategy?

NOTES

45. Consider what could go wrong

I don't believe in dwelling on the negative, in fact, I make it a point to focus on positive possibilities. However, in everything we do, we need to ask ourselves, *"What could go wrong?"* I never get in or out of a car unless it is in park. Years ago, a colleague was dropping off people at a job site. Her foot slipped off the clutch as her truck was idling in gear. The truck lurched just a little before the engine died. However, it was enough to knock the person exiting the vehicle to the ground. Fortunately, he wasn't hurt seriously. If the driver or occupant had considered what could go have gone wrong in that situation, the accident could have been avoided.

When I get out of the car with litter to toss in the garbage can, I never have my car keys in the same hand as the trash I'm throwing away (no matter how well I'm holding the keys). On the off-chance my keys could end up in the trash, I grasp them securely in my other hand. Also, when I'm getting things out of the car trunk, I never allow my keys to cross into the trunk space. So far, I've never had to dig my keys out of the trash can at the minimart, and I've never locked my keys in the trunk. However, I know people who have done both.

Always consider what could go wrong. Even though chances of a problem are not great, is it worth taking the chance? Prevention is a smart way to minimize misfortune.

Think about instances where you might have, asked, "What could go wrong?" What small action can you take in the future to avoid the risk?

Each day look for one opportunity to ask, "What could go wrong?" and take the action needed to avoid the risk completely.

NOTES

46. Trust but verify

We want others to trust us, and we need to trust others. However, you don't have to trust blindly; and there are many situations where you shouldn't. The phrase *"trust but verify"* comes from the energy industry's safety practices where hazard controls (e.g., lock and tag) are essential for preventing accidents, fatalities, environmental contamination, or destruction of expensive equipment. We read about accidents almost daily, such as electrocutions, oil refinery explosions, and industrial machinery accidents. Often the accidents can be traced back to the wrong breaker or a valve locked-out, or a worker who knew it was locked out yesterday but didn't check it again today. Although you trust that another worker locked it out correctly, you must verify it yourself. It's not that you think the other person is incompetent; it's just smart to double check, i.e., verify, given the consequences of an error.

The same philosophy can be applied to your bookkeeping, bank deposits, customer follow-up, report submittals, or vehicle maintenance. People make honest mistakes. Thus, when you can't afford the consequences, trust them to do what they should have done, but verify as needed. I used to work 30 miles from town, making a daily 60-mile round trip to work. There were no gas stations along the way. If my teenager told me she would fill the car with gas the night before, I would trust her to do it; but I'd be a fool not to verify before leaving town.

What are three things that you trust someone to do, but the consequences are such that you need to verify completeness or correctness for yourself?

NOTES

47. Check your assumptions

As you think about your major objectives, verify your assumptions. Ask yourself: *Why am I doing it? What's the purpose? Why am I approaching it this way? Is this the only way? Why am I assuming the things I'm assuming? Are my assumptions true and valid? Can I verify rather than assume?* It's important to check and verify our assumptions because often we get myopic, i.e., tunnel vision, once we have developed an idea or solution.

Once I had a project with a major milestone to start up a new plutonium waste processing plant by March 31. We assumed that the readiness of every single system was required for startup of the entire plant; and we were having a hard time doing everything needed to make the deadline. The likelihood of successfully starting everything by the deadline was minuscule. My boss (Bill), who was one of my all-times greatest mentors, asked, *"Does every system have to be ready for successful startup? Is that an accurate assumption?"*

In talking with the regulators for our industry, I found out they would accept a staggered, phased approach for the plant startup. We could start the front half of the plant where we received, assayed, x-rayed, and stored transuranic waste drums. A few months later, we could bring online the other part of the plant where we opened, sorted, and repackaged waste drums. We didn't change the milestone. We only defined it more clearly with very different assumptions.

Periodically, challenge yourself, your approach, and your assumptions. It can be an eye-opening means to your success.

What are two assumptions you are making now that you could verify or disprove? How will you check them and by when?

NOTES

48. Learn a new skill

Highly effective people are perpetually learning new skills and are open to new ideas. What skill are you learning, improving, or perfecting right now? You should always be ready to learn – no standing still or "holding your own." You're either going forward or you're going backward. The world is always expanding and moving forward; so if you're not moving forward, you're losing ground.

Are you as great as you want to be at selling your proposals, positions, or ideas? Are you as comfortable as you'd like to be speaking in front of groups? Are you the best negotiator you know? Can you facilitate a workshop as well as you like? Can you plan, organize, and execute things as effectively as you like?

Pick one or two areas where you would like to improve or grow new skills in a year's time. Develop a plan of action, and get started. For example, you could join Toastmasters to improve your speaking skills and level of comfortable in front of an audience. You could use The Great Courses (www.thegreatcourses.com), which offers audio and video formats for all kinds of learning – from critical thinking to decision making to argumentation skills and more. You could order audio books from any number of providers and listen while you commute to and from work.

Decide what skill you want to enhance and develop a plan. Will it require that you join an organization, e.g. Toastmasters, order an audiobook, or sign up for a class? Set a date, within a week, for taking action and getting started.

NOTES

49. Prepare for your next big opportunity

What is the next big opportunity for you? Is it speaking to a group of your peers at the annual association meeting, publishing a technical paper, writing a book, or pursuing a high-profile project?

Whatever it is, what can you do now to prepare for the opportunity? Or what can you do to increase chances of the opportunity materializing? If your objective is to be a presenter at the annual conference of your peers, you could speak at smaller events now to give yourself practice and exposure. You could participate in a speaking group such as Toastmasters or volunteer to speak at Rotary or Kiwanis meetings.

Identifying and tapping into a mentor may help you prepare. Have you identified a mentor who has done what you want to accomplish? You could take your mentor to lunch and ask for advice.

Are you reading or listening to books on the topic? Are you putting aside money per a plan to be in a position to act when the time comes?

What is the next big opportunity you want for yourself? What are the top three things you could do to prepare for the opportunity? Schedule the actions required to get things moving.

NOTES

50. Make incremental improvements

Brian Tracy said. *"You should strive to become one half of one percent more effective every day."* In other words, no one ever lost 100 pounds. Instead, he or she lost 1 pound 100 times. I recently set a goal to complete 100 pushups without stopping. I started with a comfortable number of pushups I knew I could complete without fail. Then, every day I added just one more. I reasoned that, if I did 30 pushups yesterday, then surely I could do 31 today. And so it went until I reached 100. If I'd waited until I was ready to do 100, I never would have started.

Here's how you can focus on incremental improvement. For each of the important areas of your life, ask yourself: What can I do today that will allow me to be slightly better than I was yesterday? It may require five extra minutes on the treadmill, paying an extra $25.00 on a credit card bill, or making one extra call to a potential client.

In the Malaysian culture, only the gods are considered capable of producing anything perfectly. Whenever Malaysians make something, they purposely incorporate a flaw so the gods will not be offended. Although, some things need to be as perfect as possible, requiring extra attention to detail, perfectionism can be a form of procrastination. So accept the fact you are flawed and just start where you are now.

In what area do you want to make long-term improvements? What small but regular improvements can you make that will add up over the next three months? How will you track the improvements? Who can help hold you accountable? When will you start? Write down what you will do and when you will start.

Epilog

Now that you've read the book, no doubt, some tips resonated with you and some did not. No problem. Take the ones that work for you, practice them, incorporate them into your life, and leave the rest. Even if just a few of the tips help you become a better parent, boss, leader, manager, friend, or neighbor, the cumulative improvement over the rest of your life could be astronomical. It's like the eighth wonder of the world – compound interest.

Learn something new, take action, ask for feedback, make improvements, and repeat. It's a simple process that leads to more success. Don't ever stop.